INNER POWER
Meditations

Asherah Books
London

INNER POWER
Meditations

The Meditations that launched Calm, iTunes App of The Year 2017, and the Secret of their Origin...

Cher Chevalier

Asherah Books
London

Published by Asherah Books, 2019

The rights of Cher Chevalier as author have been asserted in
accordance with the Copyright, Designs and Patents Act, 1988.

A CIP catalogue record for this book is available from the British Library.

Paperback ISBN 978-1-909187-98-6
Ebook ISBN 978-1-909187-99-3

CONTENTS

INTRODUCTION

This book includes the original twenty four (8x3) Meditations that launched Calm, iTunes App of The Year 2017.

Cher Chevalier wrote this *INNER POWER MEDITATIONS* book to share not only her lifelong respect for meditation practices but also to reveal the secret origin of the Meditations herein to the rest of the world.

The author, Cher Chevalier is a world-renowned Spiritual Adviser, Co-Creator of PAWS - The Policy for Animal Welfare Scheme which was launched in the House of Commons co-hosted by vegetarian Henry Smith MP, Writer and Co-Creator of The Compassion In Commerce Training Program, Co-Creator of The #HANDSOFF Anti-Violence Campaign, Co-Writer of the "LOST CHILD" Song to end violence against children, Founder and CEO of Animals Actually Ltd, and in addition to this book is also Author of the following 32 books: *Compassion In Commerce, INNER JOURNEY MEDITATIONS with Cher Chevalier & Liz Solari, The Hidden Secrets of a MODERN SEER, The Hidden Truths of a MODERN SEER, The Hidden Life of a MODERN SEER, SLIM: Step Lightly In Mind, Body, Spirit,* and *ANIMALS ACTUALLY A-Z for children.*

Cher's Animals Actually books have been turned into an online game and are in development for a Hollywood movie. She has co-created a number of new technology concepts, including for some of the most famous global tech companies and has submitted groundbreaking digital policy recommendations to governments and politicians around the world. Cher was born in England into a family that boasts four generations of vegetarians and vegans. She endured near death experiences in childhood, after which her supernatural and mystical experiences began. Cher has worked as a Spiritual Adviser for over 25 years and appeared on many mainstream TV shows. She has been featured in numerous publications and radio shows around the globe. Cher was the Spiritual Adviser on the UNLOCKED movie; she was also hired to help launch the Matt Damon/Clint Eastwood movie HEREAFTER. Cher trained for 7 years with a Spiritual Master and leads a devotional life.

"May all the meditations in this little book continue to assist and empower all beings on their inner journey to The Divine."

Love and blessings,
Cher

www.spiritualadviser.co.uk

CHAPTER 1

Anxiety Release Meditations

ANXIETY RELEASE MEDITATION
(2 minutes)

Welcome to this 2-minute session for Anxiety Release.

With eyes closed, sit comfortably... And we'll begin.

Keeping the body still and the mind quiet... Take two deep, slow breaths.

With each exhale, feel all tension begin to release from the mind and body...

As you breathe deeply, practice smiling...

Keep the mind completely still... Smile! :)

Once again, breathe deeply.

You are eternal spirit; free yourself from emotions that limit.

Peace lies at your core. Happiness is a spiritual law.

Continue to breathe slowly and deeply as you feel clear-headed and relaxed.

Take one more deep breath.

Be aware of your Inner Calm. You may tap into this at any time.

Always wish yourself and others well.

Bring your attention back to the here and now, and open your eyes.

ANXIETY RELEASE MEDITATION
(5 minutes)

Welcome to this 5-minute session for Anxiety Release.

With eyes closed, sit comfortably... And we'll begin.

Keeping the body still and the mind quiet... Take three deep, slow breaths.

With each exhale, feel all tension begin to release from the mind and body...

Focus your attention on the base of your spine...

As you keep your focus here for a few moments, breathing deeply... Practice smiling...

Keep the mind completely still... Focus on smiling...

Now take your breath even deeper.

Take your attention to your feelings of anxiety... Feel your anxiety rise in your body now...
Face it.

Take another deep breath.

Remember to smile! :)

Now locate where your anxiety sits in your body... Keep your attention there.
Give your anxiety a colour... Let the colour appear in your mind's eye... See it clearly...
Now send the colour waves of peace... Until the colour becomes white...

Stay focused.

With a smile on your face, take a deep breath.

You are eternal spirit; free yourself from emotions that limit.

13

Peace lies at your core. Happiness is a spiritual law.

Take another deep breath...

And take your focus back to the base of the spine.

Keep your attention there as you feel relaxed, clear-headed and happy.

Take another two deep breaths...

Be aware of your Inner Calm. You may tap into this at any time.

Always wish yourself and others well.

Bring your attention back to the here and now... and open your eyes.

ANXIETY RELEASE MEDITATION
(10 minutes)

Welcome to this 10-minute session for Anxiety Release.

With eyes closed, be sitting in a comfortable position... And we'll begin.

Keeping the body still and the mind quiet, begin to breathe slowly...

And take five deep, easy breaths.

With each exhale, feel all tension begin to release from the mind and from the body...

Focus your attention on the energy centre at the base of your spine... Keep your focus here for a few moments as you breathe deeply...

Keeping your focus on the base of your spine... Eyes closed... Breathing slowly... Practice smiling...

Keep the mind completely still... Do not allow the voices of the mind to intrude... Focus on smiling...

Now take your breath even... deeper.

Take your attention to your feelings of anxiety... Allow the vibration of anxiety rise to the surface. Feel it in your body... Face it. Face your anxiety.

Take another deep breath.

Now locate where your anxiety sits in your body... Allow your mind to be drawn to the part where your anxiety is located... Keep your attention there.

Remember to smile! :)

Now give your anxiety a colour... Let the colour appear in your mind's eye...

Focus on the colour of your emotion. See it clearly...

Now send the colour waves of peace and happiness... until the colour becomes white...

Know that you are greater than your emotions...

With a smile on your face, take 3 deep breaths.

You are eternal spirit; free yourself from emotions that limit.
Peace lies at your core. Happiness is a spiritual law.

Once again, take three deep breaths...

See yourself sitting on the grassy bank of a calm and clear stream... Place your bare feet into the water... Then both of your hands...

Breathe.

Let go your worries and woes, your fears and foes;
Let spring water bring rest and repose.

Let your anxiety release;
And your worries cease.
It's time to trust in peace.

Take a deep breath and smile!

Feel every aspect of your being... Keep your hands and feet in the water until you feel completely calm... and free from all anxiety... Smile :)

Take two deep, slow breaths now.

Take your attention back to the base of the spine. Focus here for a few moments as you feel relaxed, clear-headed and happy.

And again, take two deep breaths...

Be aware of your Inner Calm. You may tap into this at any time.

Always wish yourself and others well.

Bring your attention back to the here and now... And when you feel ready, you can open your eyes.

17

CHAPTER 2

Confidence Meditations

CONFIDENCE MEDITATION
(2 minutes)

Welcome to this 2-minute session for Confidence.

With eyes closed, sit comfortably... And we'll begin.

Keeping the body still and the mind quiet, take two deep breaths.

Let all tension release from the mind and body...

Imagine in front of you a mountain... Feel yourself stand tall as you focus on the summit...

Feeling motivated and strong, begin to climb the mountain...

Keeping the top in sight - focus on triumphing!

The higher you climb, the more you feel confident and happy!

Stay focused on the top... Walk on with power and purpose...

The top is in sight; with all your might, strive towards the peak.

Faith overcomes fear; the top is near.

With confidence know you are unique.

See yourself arrive at the peak of the mountain... Stand firm and tall...

Be fearless and triumphant!

Be aware of your Inner Strength. You may tap into this at any time.

Always wish yourself and others well.

Bring your attention back to the here and now, and open your eyes.

21

22

CONFIDENCE MEDITATION
(5 minutes)

Welcome to this 5-minute session for Confidence.

With eyes closed, sit comfortably... And we'll begin.

Keeping the body still and the mind quiet, take three deep breaths.

With each exhale, allow all tension to release from the mind and body...

Imagine in front of you a mountain... The peak rising towards the sky above...
See the mountain clearly in your mind's eye.

Keep breathing deeply, both feet firmly on the Earth... and stand tall
as you focus on the summit...

Feeling motivated and strong, stride forwards and begin to climb the mountain...

Keeping the top in sight, focus on ascension... Focus on triumphing!

The higher you climb, the more you feel yourself walking tall and HAPPY!

Stay focused on the top.

A little further along the path, you will notice a powerful being robed in white.
You feel drawn to them.

As you approach the being, they guide you to sit on a bench, side by side, and rest...

The powerful being will speak. Body still, mind silent, breathe even deeper now.

Listen closely to their every word as they say to you:

Know that all is possible.

23

Be sure that all things are achievable.

Be aware that life is eternal.

Be certain that your role is important.

Take two deep breaths.

Be ready to continue your ascent now... Walk on with power and purpose...

Take wider strides now, onwards and upwards! Keep the summit in your focus...

The top is in sight; with all your might, strive towards the peak.

Faith overcomes fear; the top is near.

With confidence know you are unique.

Take the final few steps to the top now...

See yourself arrive at the peak of the mountain...

Take deep breaths... Stand firm and tall...

Be fearless and triumphant!

Be aware of your Inner Strength. You may tap into this at any time.

Always wish yourself and others well.

Bring your attention back to the here and now, and open your eyes.

CONFIDENCE MEDITATION
(10 minutes)

Welcome to this 10-minute session for Confidence.

With eyes closed, be sitting comfortably... And we'll begin.

Keeping the body still and the mind quiet, begin to breathe deeply...
and take five deep, easy breaths.

With each exhale, let all tension begin to release from the mind and from the body...

As your body relaxes and mind calms, focus your attention on the area of your throat...
Keep your attention here for a few moments.

Imagine in front of you a mountain... The peak rising towards the sky above you...
See the mountain clearly in your mind's eye.

Keep breathing deeply, both feet firmly on the Earth... and stand tall
as you focus on the summit...

Feeling motivated and strong, start striding forwards. Begin to climb the mountain...

Keeping the top in sight, focus on ascension... Focus on triumphing!

Continue to breathe deeply in time with your steady strides.

The higher you climb, the more you feel yourself walking tall, confident, HAPPY!

Stay focused on the top of the mountain. It's getting closer.

A little further along the path, you will notice a powerful being robed in white.
You feel drawn to them.

As you approach the being, they guide you to sit on a bench, side by side, and rest...

The powerful being will speak. Body still, mind silent, breathe even deeper now.

Listen closely to their every word as they say to you:

Know that all is possible.

Be sure that all things are achievable.

Be aware that life is eternal.

Be certain that your role is unique and important.

Again...

Know that is all is possible.

Be sure that all things are achievable.

Be aware that life is eternal.

Be certain that your role is unique and important.

Take two deep breaths.

Be ready to continue your ascent now... As you take your steps, keep breathing deeply...
Walk on with power and purpose...

Take wider strides now, onwards and upwards! Keep the summit in your focus...

Embrace your destiny!... Feel your inner strength guiding you upwards...

The top is in sight; with all your might, strive towards the peak.

Faith overcomes fear; the top is near.

With confidence know you are unique.

Take the final few steps to the top now... Your goal is within reach.

See yourself arrive at the peak of the mountain...

Take deep breaths...

Now stand firm and tall.

Hear strong the call.

To shine and be your ALL.

Arms outstretched, gaze at the sky above you... Be fearless and triumphant!

With each deep breath, inhale your success and feel it vibrate through your body,
heart and mind...

Know that infinite possibilities are open to you now...

Once again, take three deep breaths.

Be aware of your Inner Strength. You may tap into this at any time.
Always wish yourself and others well.

Bring your attention back to the here and now... And when you feel ready,
you can open your eyes.

CHAPTER 3

Creativity Meditations

30

CREATIVITY MEDITATION
(2 minutes)

Welcome to this 2-minute session for Creativity.

With eyes closed, sit comfortably... And we'll begin.

Keeping the body still and the mind quiet, take two deep breaths.

Relax...

Imagine you're in the wide open countryside... Green all around...

Up ahead is a tree... Slowly walk towards it... And sit on the fresh grass beneath it...

Take two deep breaths...

Begin to look around the scene now, and connect with the inspiring nature all around you...

Place your hands on the soft grass... Sense the vibration of Earth's silent power enter through your palms and move up to your heart... Feel the creative energy filling your heart!

The creative forces are eternal and true.

The well of wonders lies within you.

Take another deep breath...

Be aware of your deep well of Inner Inspiration. You may tap into this at any time.

Always wish yourself and others well.

Bring your attention back to the here and now... And open your eyes.

CREATIVITY MEDITATION
(5 minutes)

Welcome to this 5-minute session for Creativity.

With eyes closed, sit comfortably... And we'll begin.

Keeping the body still and the mind quiet, begin to take three deep breaths.

With each exhale, feel all tension release from the mind and body...

As your body relaxes and your mind calms, focus your attention on your heart and keep it there for a few moments...

Imagine you're in the wide open countryside. It's green all around...

Up ahead is a tree... Slowly walk towards the tree... And sit down comfortably on the green grass beneath it...

Take two deep, easy breaths...

Begin to look around the scene now, and connect with the inspiring nature all around you...

Place your hands on the soft grass... Sense the vibration of Earth's silent power enter through your palms and move up to your heart.

Now slowly lift your hands... move your body... and place both hands on the trunk of the tree...

Sense the natural strength of the tree as you feel calmer inside your Self and continue to breathe deeply.

The creative forces are eternal and true.

The well of wonders lies within you.

Take another deep breath...

And one more...

Now take your attention high into the sky and see a rainbow there... Feel inspired gazing at its bright hues forming an arc above you...

Use your imagination to be open to what the seven colours can teach you...

Red - vitality

Orange - creativity

Yellow - joy

Green - growth

Blue - confidence

Indigo - inspiration

Violet - purpose.

This flow of light and insight is your birthright.

Once again, take two deep, easy breaths...

Take your attention back to your heart... Feel the creative energy filling your heart!

Be aware of your deep well of Inner Inspiration. You may tap into this at any time.

Always wish yourself and others well.

Bring your attention back to the here and now... And open your eyes.

CREATIVITY MEDITATION
(10 minutes)

Welcome to this 10-minute session for Creativity.

With eyes closed, settle into a comfortable seated position... And we'll begin.

Keeping the body still and the mind quiet, begin to breathe slowly...

Take five deep, easy breaths.

With each exhale, feel all tension begin to release from the mind and from the body...

As your body relaxes and your mind calms, focus your attention on the area around your heart...

Keep your attention here for a few moments...

Now imagine you're in the wide open countryside. It's green all around... Up ahead is a tree...

Slowly... walk towards the tree...

When you reach it, you sit down comfortably on the green grass...

Breathe... Take three deep, easy breaths...

Begin to look around the scene now, and connect with the inspiring nature all around you...

Place your hands, palms down on the soft grass... Sense the vibration of Earth's silent power enter through your hands and move up through your arms to your heart.

Let your fingers reach for a leaf now on the ground next to you... and hold it... Explore how the leaf feels fresh between your fingers...

Look closer at its natural shape and patterns.

Now slowly lift your hands... move your body... and place both hands on the trunk of the tree. Stay here for a moment...

Sense the natural strength and solidity of the tree as you feel more and more calm and centred inside your Self...

Keep the mind still as you continue to take deep breaths...

The creative forces are eternal and true.

The well of wonders lies within you.

Take another deep breath...

And another...

And one more.

Now take your attention high into the sky and see a rainbow there...

Feel happy and inspired gazing at its bright hues forming an arc far above you...

Use your imagination to be open to what the seven colours can teach you...

Red - strength and vitality

Orange - enthusiasm and creativity

Yellow - wisdom and joy

Green - growth and harmony

Blue - peace and confidence

Indigo - intuition and inspiration

Violet - purpose and healing.

This flow of light and insight is your birthright.

Once again, take three deep breaths...

Take your attention back to your heart... Feel the creative energy filling your heart!

Be aware of your deep well of Inner Inspiration. You may tap into this at any time.

Always wish yourself and others well.

Bring your attention back to the here and now... And open your eyes.

CHAPTER 4

Energy Meditations

ENERGY MEDITATION
(2 minutes)

Welcome to this 2-minute session for Energy.

With eyes closed, sit comfortably... And we'll begin.

Keeping the body still and the mind quiet, take two deep, easy breaths.

With each exhale, allow all tension to release from the mind and body...

Imagine in front of you a curved wooden bridge over a calm pond.
Across the bridge is a waterfall.

You will notice, to your left, a powerful being robed in white.
They guide you safely across the bridge.

Arriving at the waterfall, your guide shows you to a white marble step to stand on within the water. Step on to it with confidence.

Let the water flow freely over you.

Allow the water to wash away tiredness, doubt, anger and blame.

Positive energy flow is your aim.

Take another deep breath and on the exhalation, leave the waterfall feeling energised!

The powerful being robed in white will guide you along a path to a gate.
Walk through the gate feeling enthusiastic and empowered!

Be aware of your Inner Power. You may tap into this at any time.

Always wish yourself and others well.

Bring your attention back to the here and now, and open your eyes.

ENERGY MEDITATION
(5 minutes)

Welcome to this 5-minute session for Energy.

With eyes closed, be sitting in a comfortable position... And we'll begin.

Keeping the body still and the mind quiet, begin to breathe slowly...
take three deep, easy breaths.

With each exhale, feel all tension begin to release from the mind and body... relax.

Focus your attention on the area of your stomach just above the belly button...
Keep your focus here for a few moments...

Now take the breath even deeper...

Imagine in front of you a curved wooden bridge over a calm pond.
Across the bridge is a waterfall.

You will notice, to your left, a powerful being robed in white. They guide you safely and slowly
across the wooden bridge to the waterfall.

Arriving at the waterfall, your guide shows you to a white marble step to stand on within the
water. Step on to it and stand confidently with your feet firmly on the marble...

Let the water flow freely over you.

Allow the water to wash away tiredness, doubt, anger and blame.
Positive energy flow is your aim.

You're feeling motivated, enthusiastic, empowered.
With vibrant energy you're being showered.

Keeping the body still and mind calm, focus now on feeling powerful waves of positive energy
flowing up through the soles of your feet to the top of your head.

43

Feel and see the positive vibrations flowing up through your soles, energising your feet...
energising your legs... energising your stomach... heart area... shoulders... arms...
hands... face... and head.

Stand tall in your own good energy.

Take two deep breaths and leave the waterfall feeling energised!

The powerful being robed in white will guide you along a path. Up ahead you see a gate.
Walk through the gate feeling invigorated!

Continue to breathe deeply...

Be aware of your Inner Power. You may tap into this at any time.

Always wish yourself and others well.

Bring your attention back to the here and now, and open your eyes.

ENERGY MEDITATION
(10 minutes)

Welcome to this 10-minute session for Energy.

With eyes closed, be sitting in a comfortable position... And we'll begin.

Keeping the body still and the mind quiet, begin to breathe slowly...
and take five deep, easy breaths.

With each exhale, feel tension begin to release from the mind and from the body...

Relax... Allow all tension to release from body and mind...

Focus your attention on the area of your stomach just above the belly button...
Keep your focus here for a moment...

Now take the breath even deeper...

Imagine in front of you a curved wooden bridge over a calm pond.
Across the bridge is a waterfall.

You will notice, to your left, a powerful being robed in white. They guide you safely, steadily,
across the wooden bridge to the waterfall.

Continue to take deep breaths as you walk slowly over the bridge together.

Arriving at the waterfall, your guide shows you to a white marble step to stand on within the
water. Step on to it and stand confidently with your feet firmly on the marble...

Let the water flow freely over you.

Allow the water to wash away tiredness, doubt, anger and blame.
Positive energy flow is your aim.

You're feeling motivated, enthusiastic, empowered.
With vibrant energy you're being showered.

Keeping the body still and the mind calm, focus now on feeling powerful waves of positive energy flowing up through the soles of your feet to the top of your head.

Feel and see the positive vibrations flowing up through your soles, energising your feet...

Feel the positive vibrations rise up and energise your ankles...

Feel the positive vibrations energise your lower legs...

knees... upper legs...

hips... stomach... heart area...

shoulders... arms... hands...

neck... jaw... cheeks...

eyes... and the whole of the head.

Stand tall in your own good energy!

Once again, take five deep breaths and at the end of the fifth breath,
you leave the waterfall feeling energised.

You leave the waterfall, and the powerful being robed in white will guide you along a path.
Up ahead you see a gate.

Walk through the gate feeling motivated and invigorated.

Continue to breathe deeply...

Be aware of your Inner Power. You may tap into this at any time.

Always wish yourself and others well.

Bring your attention back to the here and now.

When you feel ready, open your eyes.

47

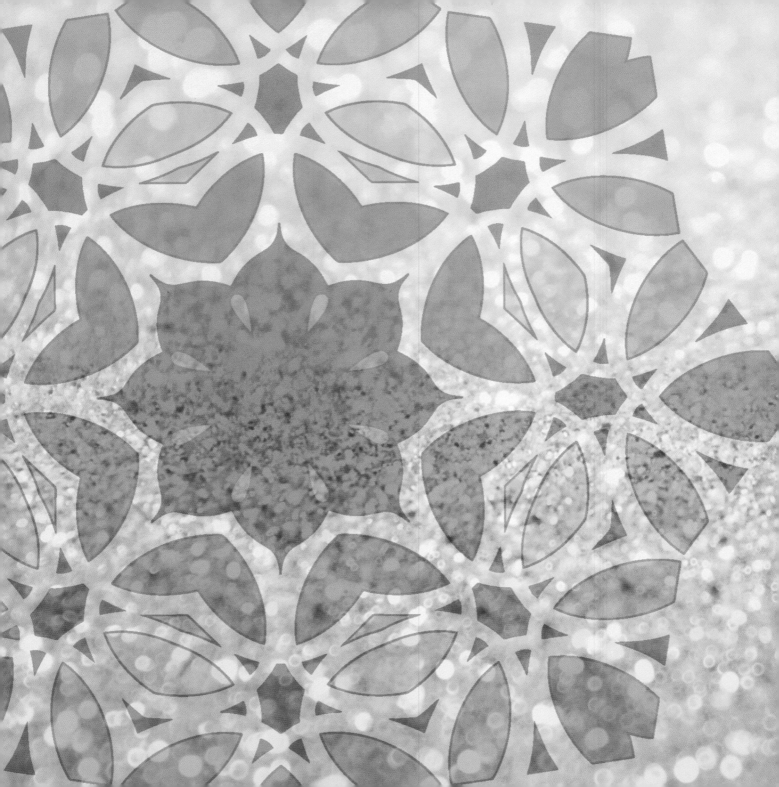

CHAPTER 5

Focus Meditations

50

FOCUS MEDITATION
(2 minutes)

Welcome to this 2-minute session for Focus.

Close your eyes... Sit comfortably... And we'll begin.

Keeping the body still and the mind quiet, begin to breathe slowly and deeply.

With each exhale, feel all tension begin to release from the mind and body...

Now bring your attention to the point between your eyebrows...

Visualise in front of you a red circle...

In your mind's eye, picture the goal you want to achieve within the red circle.
See yourself within the scene... Hold the picture firmly in your mind...

Still your thoughts, body, soul. Focus your mind on the goal.

Keep your focus like an arrow,
Aimed right at the point, straight and narrow.

Continue to hold the vision in your mind's eye until you see it complete,
your goal achieved.

Take a deep breath.

Be aware of your Inner Strength. You may tap into this at any time.

Always wish yourself and others well.

Bring your attention back to the here and now, and open your eyes.

FOCUS MEDITATION
(5 minutes)

Welcome to this 5-minute session for Focus.

Keeping the body still and the mind quiet, begin to breathe slowly...

And take three deep, easy breaths.

With each exhale, feel all tension begin to release from the mind and from the body...

Now bring your attention to the point between your eyebrows...

Visualise in front of you a red circle... Continue to breathe gently
as you focus on the red circle...

In your mind's eye, start to picture the goal you want to achieve within the red circle.

Hold the picture firmly in your mind and imagine as many details as you can about achieving
your goal. Picture yourself within the scene...

Still your thoughts, body, soul. Focus your mind on the goal.

Keep your focus like an arrow,
Aimed right at the point, straight and narrow.

Continue to hold the vision in your mind's eye.

Allow the scene to unfold until you see it complete...
Keep focused.

Deepen your breathing now, as the body rests still and calm.

Direct your thoughts, be centred, focus.

Your mind is clear and pure like a lotus.

Once again, take three deep, easy breaths.

Keep breathing deeply as you take your attention back to the energy centre between your eyebrows.

Focus.

Be aware of your Inner Strength. You may tap into this at any time.

Always wish yourself and others well.

Bring your attention back to the here and now... And open your eyes.

FOCUS MEDITATION
(10 minutes)

Welcome to this 10-minute session for Focus.

With eyes closed, be sitting in a comfortable position... And we'll begin.

Keeping the body still and the mind quiet, begin to breathe slowly...

And take five deep, easy breaths.

With each exhale, feel all tension begin to release from the mind and from the body...

Relax...

Now bring your attention to the point between your eyebrows,
directly above the nose.

Continuing to breathe slowly as you keep your attention here for a few moments...

Visualise a red circle in front of you. See a red circle as clearly as you can...

In your mind's eye, start to picture the goal you want to focus on and achieve
within the red circle.

See your goal come to life within the circle.

Hold the picture firmly in your mind...
And imagine as many details as you can about achieving your goal.

See what happens...

Imagine your success happening... Picture yourself within the scene...

Still your thoughts, body, soul. Focus your mind on the goal.

Keep your focus like an arrow,
Aimed right at the point, straight and narrow.
Continue to hold your vision firmly in your mind's eye...

Allow the scene to unfold until you see your goal achieved and complete...

Hold the vision. Stay focused.

Deepen your breathing now, as the body rests still and the mind silent.

Direct your thoughts, be centred, focus.

Your mind is clear and pure like a lotus.

Once again, take five deep breaths.

Up ahead is a lotus pond. See yourself take steady steps towards it...
and seat yourself comfortably on the bank...

As you sit beside the lotus pond, keep the body still and the mind silent...

Focus steadfastly on the stillness of the water before you...
Keep your attention on the water...

With clarity and determination, focus your mind again on your goal.
See your vision complete and whole.

Now, with confidence and surety of mind, leave the lotus pond behind.

Take another five deep breaths.

Keep breathing deeply as you take your attention back to the energy centre
between your eyebrows. Focus here...

Know you are centred and have clarity of mind.

Be aware of your Inner Strength. You may tap into this at any time.

Always wish yourself and others well.

Bring your attention back to the here and now...

And when you feel ready, you can open your eyes.

CHAPTER 6

Inner Peace Meditations

INNER PEACE MEDITATION
(2 minutes)

Welcome to this 2-minute session for Inner Peace.

Close your eyes, sit comfortably, and we'll begin.

Keeping the body still and the mind quiet, take two deep, slow breaths.

With each exhale, feel all tension release from the mind and body...

Imagine before you a beautiful sunny beach and a calm blue ocean... Sense the warm sand beneath your feet as you walk slowly barefoot towards the shore.

You arrive at the water's edge now, feeling peaceful,
and sit comfortably on the soft sand...

Focus your gaze on the serene sunset as you continue to breathe rhythmically.

Your mind is still, as you release your will.
Your worries cease; be at peace.
Rest now in healing harmony,
Know this is your rightful destiny.

Take another deep breath.

See yourself get up from the sand and calmly leave the beach behind...

Again, take a deep, relaxing breath.

Be aware of your powerful Inner Peace... You may tap into this at any time.

Always wish yourself and others well.

Bring your attention back to the here and now, and open your eyes.

INNER PEACE MEDITATION
(5 minutes)

Welcome to this 5-minute session for Inner Peace.

Close your eyes, sit comfortably... and we'll begin.

Keeping the body still and the mind quiet, take three deep, slow breaths.

With each exhale, feel all tension release from the mind and body...

As you continue to breathe deeply, focus now on your heart.

Imagine before you a beautiful sunny beach and a clear blue ocean...
Sense the warm, soft sand beneath your feet...

Notice how calm the ocean is...

Feel rested in the luxury of having this sunny, silent place all to yourself.

Continue to breathe deeply as you walk slowly barefoot towards the shore.

You arrive at the water's edge now, feeling peaceful...
Sit down comfortably on the warm sand...

Keeping the body still and the mind quiet, focus your gaze on the serene sunset...

As you gaze at the sunset, begin to breathe deeply in time with the rhythmic lapping
of the ocean waves...

Inhale as the tide comes gently in... Exhale as the tide flows back to the ocean...

Go deeply into and enjoy this blissful state.

Forgive yourself and all others for anything you may be harbouring...

Allow peace to flow.

Know that your true nature is total tranquillity.

Your mind is still, as you release your will.
Your worries cease; be at peace.
Rest now in healing harmony,
Know this is your rightful destiny.

Take another deep breath.

See yourself get up from the sand and calmly leave the beach behind...

Take two relaxing breaths.

Be aware of your powerful Inner Peace... You may tap into this at any time.

Always wish yourself and others well.

Bring your attention back to the here and now, and open your eyes.

INNER PEACE MEDITATION
(10 minutes)

Welcome to this 10-minute session for Inner Peace.

With eyes closed, be sitting comfortably... And we'll begin.

Keeping the body still and the mind quiet, take four deep, slow breaths.

With each exhale, feel all tension begin to release from the mind and from the body...

As you continue to breathe deeply and easily, focus on the area around your heart.

Imagine before you a beautiful sunny beach and a clear blue ocean...
Sense the warm, soft sand beneath your feet...

Notice how calm the ocean is...

Feel rested in the luxury of having this sunny, silent place all to yourself.

Continue to breathe deeply as you walk slowly barefoot through the warm sand,
towards the shore.

You arrive at the water's edge now, feeling calm and peaceful...
Sit down comfortably on the sand.

Keeping the body still and the mind quiet, focus your gaze on the serene sunset...

As you gaze at the light of the sunset, begin to breathe deeply in time with the rhythmic lapping
of the ocean waves...

Inhale as the tide comes gently in... Exhale as the tide flows back to the ocean...

Go deeply into and enjoy this blissful state.

Forgive yourself and all others for anything you may be harbouring...
Allow peace to flow.

Once more, take your attention to your heart... Feel peace filling your heart...

Know that your true nature is total tranquillity.

Your mind is still, as you release your will.
Your worries cease; be at peace.
Rest now in healing harmony,
Know this is your rightful destiny.

Once more, take a deep breath.

See yourself slowly get up from the sand...
and begin to walk peacefully along the shore again...

Slowly you stop and stand to gaze once more at the vast calmness of the ocean...
Take a deep breath...

When you're ready, you will draw the word 'PEACE' in the sand...
Visualise yourself drawing the letters p-e-a-c-e in the sand beneath your feet...

Feel the peace in your heart flowing out through your arms and hands,
guiding your movements...

See yourself continue your contented journey along the shore now
and calmly leave the beach behind.

Take two deep, relaxing breaths.

Be aware of your powerful Inner Peace... You may tap into this at any time.

Always wish yourself and others well.

Bring your attention back to the here and now...
And when you feel ready, open your eyes.

CHAPTER 7

Positivity Meditations

POSITIVITY MEDITATION
(2 minutes)

Welcome to this 2-minute session for Positivity.

With eyes closed, sit comfortably. And we'll begin.

Keeping the body still and the mind quiet, take four rhythmic, energetic breaths.

Feel positive energy pulsing through your body.

Imagine you're running through a desert... See the wide open space before you...

Feel the vastness all around...

And the heat warm on your skin as you keep on running...

Feel your heartbeat getting faster, sending positive pulsations all through your body...

Keep running... Pick up the pace... Run!

You see an oasis. Jump straight in - NO hesitation!

Get out of the water and lay on your back on the soft sand...

Gaze up at the sun...

Sense the sun's powerful energy radiating through your body... from your feet... to your legs...
stomach... and heart... to your head.

Be at one; feel the sun.
You're here, you're alive.
You're sure to thrive.

Take 2 energising breaths.

Now get up and RUN! GO FOR IT!

Up ahead you notice a road.

See yourself arrive, step on to it and stand strong on the tarmac...

Look behind you... Look in front of you... Your path ahead is clear.

Be aware of your Inner Power. You may tap into this at any time.

Always wish yourself and others well.

Bring your attention back to the here and now... And open your eyes.

POSITIVITY MEDITATION
(5 minutes)

Welcome to this 5-minute session for Positivity.

With eyes closed, sit comfortably. And we'll begin.

Keeping the body still and the mind quiet, take five energetic breaths.

Breathe rhythmically yet quickly.

Feel positive energy pulsing through your body.

Imagine now that you're running through a desert...

See the wide open space before you...

Feel the vastness all around...

Sense the heat warm on your skin as you keep on running...

Feel your heartbeat getting faster, sending positive pulsations all through your body...

Keep running... Revel in the freedom of having all this light open space to yourself...

Pick up the pace... Run! Run for it!

You see an oasis. Race to it and jump straight in - NO hesitation!

Get out of the water and lay on your back on the soft,
warm sand and gaze up at the sun...

As you continue to gaze upwards, sense the sun's powerful energy radiating through your body... Feel it flowing up through the soles of your feet... to your legs... your stomach... your heart... your arms... your face... to the top of your head.

Take 3 more rhythmic breaths.

Be at one; feel the sun.

You're here, you're alive.

You're sure to thrive.

There are no limits here.

The road ahead is clear.

Once more, take 3 breaths.

Feel the life-force. You are on course.

Take another 2 energising breaths.

Give thanks to the Divine for this positivity boost.

Now get up and start running!

Pick up the pace again and RUN!

Keep running through the desert, feeling more alive and energised with each stride!

Up ahead you notice a road. Head straight for it...

See yourself arrive at the verge, step on to it and stand strong on the tarmac...

Look behind you... Look in front of you... Your path ahead is clear.

Take 2 more breaths.

Choose your path...

With the power of goodness in your heart.

GO FOR IT!

Again, take 2 energising breaths.

Feel the positive energy pumping through your body!

Be aware of your Inner Power. You may tap into this at any time. Always wish
yourself and others well.

Bring your attention back to the here and now... And open your eyes.

POSITIVITY MEDITATION
(10 minutes)

Welcome to this 10-minute session for Positivity.

With eyes closed, be sitting in a comfortable position... And we'll begin.

Keeping the body still and the mind quiet, begin to breathe quickly...
Take six energetic breaths. Breathe rhythmically yet quickly.

Feel positive energy pulsing through your body.

Imagine now that you're running through a desert...

See the wide open space before you...

Feel the vast space all around...

Sense the heat warm on your skin as you keep on running...

Feel your heartbeat getting faster, sending positive pulsations all through your body...
from your feet to the top of your head.

Keep running... Revel in the freedom of having all this light open space to yourself...

Pick up the pace... Run!

Run for the fun of it!

You see an oasis. Race to it and jump straight in - NO hesitation!

Get out of the water and lay on your back on the soft, warm sand...

Gaze up at the sun above...

As you continue to gaze upwards, sense the sun's powerful energy radiating through your
body... Feel it flowing up through the soles of your feet... to your lower legs... your knees...

your thighs... your stomach... your heart... your arms... your hands... your throat... your mouth...
your face... your eyes... your forehead...
to the top of your head.

Take 4 more rhythmic breaths.

Be at one; feel the sun.
You're here, you're alive.
You're sure to thrive.

There are no limits here.
The road ahead is clear.

Once more, take 4 breaths.

Sit up and focus your attention on the oasis...

Move and bring yourself to the water's edge...

With both hands, drink the pure water.

Feel the life-force.
You are on course.

Take another 3 energising breaths.

Give thanks to the Divine for this positivity boost.

Now get up and start running!

Pick up the pace again and RUN!

You're on track. Never look back!

Keep running through the wide open desert, feeling more and more alive
and energised with each stride!

Up ahead you notice a road. Head straight for it...

See yourself arrive at the verge of the road and step on to it.

Stand strong on the tarmac...

Look behind you... Look in front of you...Your path ahead is clear.

Take three more breaths.

Feel the life-force.
You are on course.
There are no limits here.
The road ahead is clear.

Choose your path...

With the power of goodness in your heart.

GO FOR IT!

Again, take 6 energising breaths.

Feel the positive energy pumping through your body!

Be aware of your Inner Power. You may tap into this at any time.

Always wish yourself and others well.

Bring your attention back to the here and now... And when you feel ready,
you can open your eyes.

79

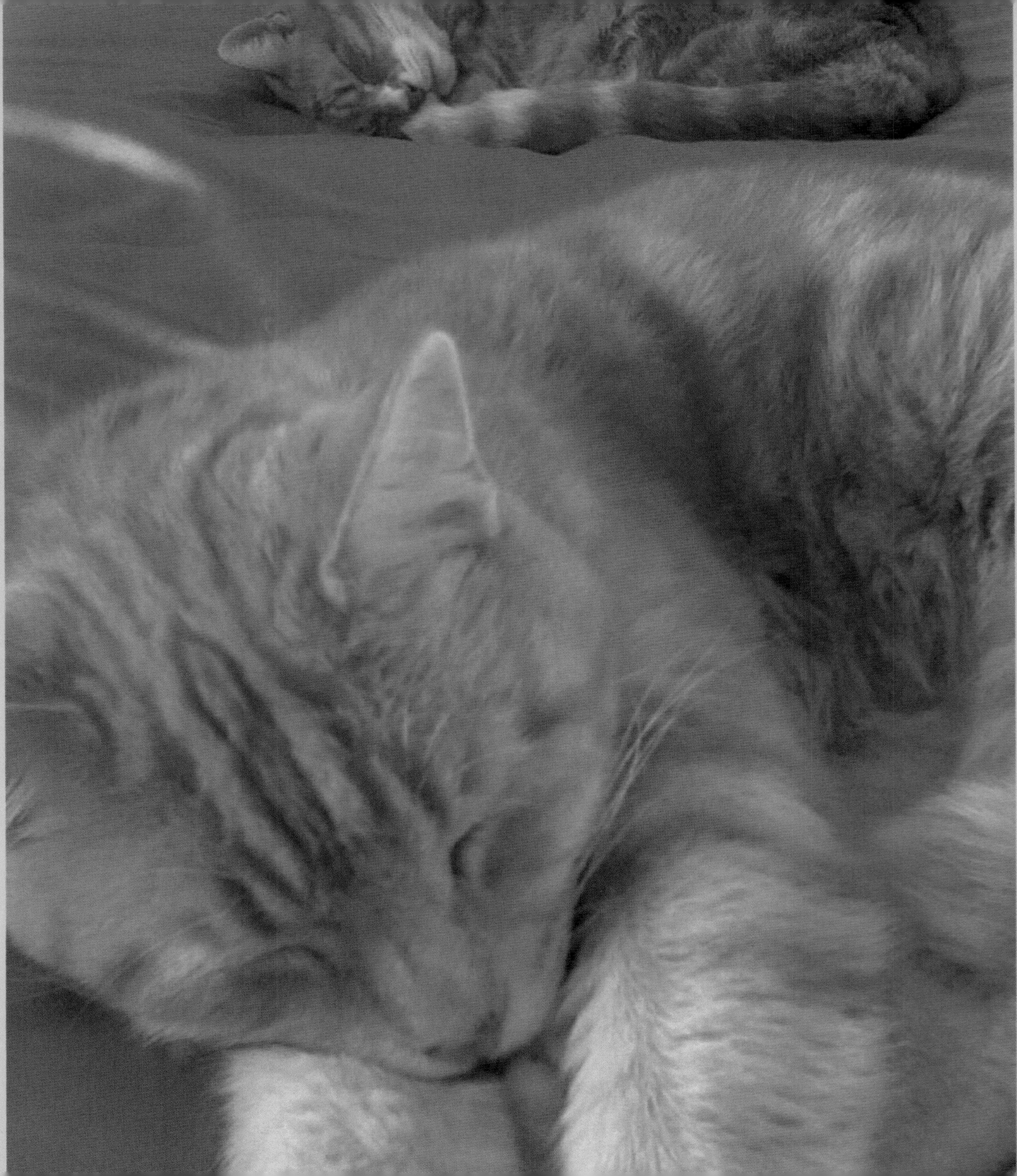

CHAPTER 8

Sleep Meditations

SLEEP MEDITATION
(2 minutes)

Welcome to this 2-minute session for Sleep.

With eyes closed, sit or lie down comfortably... And we'll begin.

Keeping the body still and the mind quiet... Take two slow, gentle breaths.

With each exhale, feel all tension begin to release from the mind and body...

Visualise yourself inside your special peaceful place... A cosy wood cabin within a beautiful forest... It's dusk and quiet.

The glow of candlelight mingles with the embers of an open fire...

Know you are safe inside this beautiful place.

Continue to take slow, gentle breaths...

In front of you is a giant sand-coloured cushion... And a big, furry orange blanket...

Position yourself slowly onto the soft comfortable cushion...
And get snug beneath the thick blanket...

Relax your legs... Relax your stomach... Relax your arms... Relax your face...

Sleepiness flows over you...

The candle wick burns out...

In total peacefulness...

Pure and deep...

I leave you now to rest and sleep.

SLEEP MEDITATION
(5 minutes)

Welcome to this 5-minute session for Sleep.

With eyes closed, sit or lie down comfortably... And we'll begin.

Keeping the body still and the mind quiet... Take three slow, gentle breaths.

With each exhale, feel all tension begin to release from the mind and body...

Visualise yourself being inside your special peaceful place... A cosy wood cabin within a beautiful forest... It's dusk and quiet.

The glow of candlelight mingles with the warming embers of an open fire... All around, the forest rests completely silent.

Know you are safe inside this beautiful place.

Continue to take slow, gentle breaths...

Take off your shoes now... Feel the warmth of the floor beneath your feet...

In front of you is a giant sand-coloured cushion... And a big, furry orange blanket...

Position yourself slowly onto the giant cushion... Feel enveloped by its soft comfort as you get snug beneath the thick blanket...

Gently wriggle your toes as, in the background, you hear the embers of the fire burning in the grate...

Relax...

Your body feels light...

Feel every part of your body relaxing as you take slow gentle breaths...

Relax your feet... Relax your legs... Relax your stomach... Relax your arms... Relax your face...

Sleepiness flows over you...

Take 2 more gentle breaths.

Release all thoughts...

Forgive yourself and all others...

Be completely peaceful and rested.

The candle wick burns out...

Feel safe and warm in the velvety darkness.

Let your consciousness rest in blissful calmness.

Take another three slow, very gentle breaths...

In total peacefulness...

Pure and deep...

I leave you now to rest and sleep.

SLEEP MEDITATION
(10 minutes)

Welcome to this 10-minute session for Sleep.

With eyes closed, be seated or lying comfortably... And we'll begin.

Keeping the body still and the mind quiet, begin to breathe slowly...
And take five slow, gentle breaths.

With each exhale, feel all tension begin to release from the mind and from the body...

Visualise yourself being inside your special peaceful place... A cosy wood cabin within a
beautiful forest... It's dusk and quiet.

The glow of candlelight mingles with the warming embers of an open fire...
It's quiet, and all around, the forest rests completely silent.

Know you are safe inside this beautiful place.

Continue to take slow, gentle breaths...

Carefully take off your shoes now... And place them near the fire... Feel the warmth of the
floor beneath your feet...

In front of you is a giant sand-coloured cushion... And a big, furry orange blanket...

Position yourself slowly onto the giant cushion... Feel enveloped by its soft comfort as you get
snug beneath the thick, furry blanket...

Take 3 gentle breaths.

Gently wriggle your toes as, in the background, you hear the embers of the fire
burning in the grate...

Relax...

87

Your body feels light, almost weightless...

Feel every part of your body relaxing in total peacefulness as you take slow gentle breaths...

Relax your feet... Relax your legs... Relax your stomach... Relax your arms and hands...
Relax your shoulders... Relax your jaw... Relax your face... Relax your head...

Sleepiness flows over you...

Slumber most comfortably,
Be restful and peaceful,
Sleep harmoniously.

Take 3 more gentle breaths.

Release all thoughts... Let everything go... Be gentle.
Forgive yourself and all others.
Be completely peaceful and rested.

Look forward now to harmonious dreams.
Soothing slumber is closer than it seems.

The candlelight dims and the wick burns out...

Feel safe and warm in the velvety darkness.
Let your consciousness rest in blissful calmness.

Once again, take five slow, very gentle breaths...

In total peacefulness...

Pure and deep...

I leave you now to rest and sleep.

CHAPTER 9

The Secret Origin

GOD
and
TWO WOMEN

It is with humility that I ask the reader to bear with me as I do my best to reveal the secret origin and explain with brevity and in ordinary language what is ineffable.

Since suffering near-death-experiences in early childhood I have had what can only be described as mystical moments of oneness, attunement if you will, with Angelic Helpers, Masters, and even Yeshua/Jesus Himself; leading ultimately to my living a devotional life in union with GOD.

From the Autumn of 2012 through to early Spring of 2013 my student Maggie Richards and I discussed this project for Calm. I pray and meditate daily - practices I have adhered to for more than twenty five years - and during my prayers and meditations as well as dreams and visions throughout this period, GOD imparted the words of these said 24 (8x3) Meditations to me.

In my humble and honest opinion, GOD and two women, namely myself and my meditation student Maggie Richards, wrote the content that launched Calm.

For reference, Maggie Richards is now a Meditation Teacher, Founder of Smiley Minds relaxation resources for kids, and author of *A Guide to Being a Better Being*.

Here is a brief timeline of how and when the content that launched Calm was created:

October 2012

Cher Chevalier assists one of her meditation students, Maggie Richards in writing: The 7 Steps of Calm.

November 2012

Cher Chevalier is guided by GOD to select and suggest another of her meditation students, Natasha Beaumont to be the voiceover artist of the Meditations that Calm will launch their App with.

March 2013

The Calm App launches with:
The 7 Steps of Calm.

Maggie Richards begins writing ideas for eight Meditations for Calm but she is not confident that her ideas are good enough and so asks her Meditation Teacher, Cher Chevalier to help her.

Cher Chevalier prays over it, and then agrees.

April 2013

Cher Chevalier re-writes Maggie Richards' attempts at the Meditations for Calm, ensuring that the words GOD imparted to her are used - as they are for the upliftment of humanity and the glorification of GOD. Cher Chevalier then emails the final 24 (8x3) Meditations that Calm will launch their app with.

Cher Chevalier retains all her original emails containing these Meditations - the last one of which she emailed to Maggie Richards states the following:

"Be thankful to 'those' who have shared the words to make the meditations complete. I pray we have done them justice - being merely a vessel for them to work through in this dimension. God Bless."

May 2013

Calm launch the 24 (8x3) Meditations on their app.

"In Meditation may you find GOD"

NOTES

NOTES

_____

_____

_____

_____

_____

_____

_____

_____

_____

_____

_____

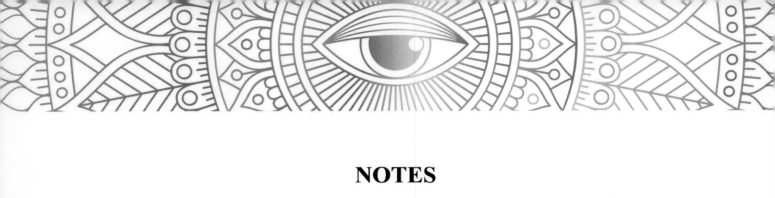

NOTES

NOTES

_____

_____

_____

_____

_____

_____

_____

_____

_____

_____

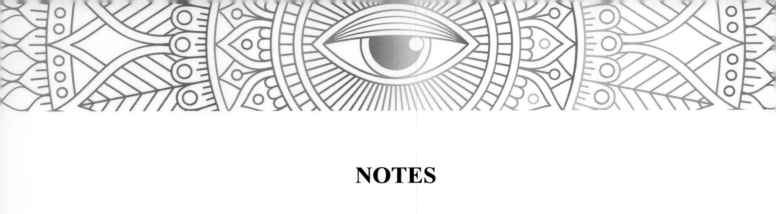

NOTES

_____

_____

_____

_____

_____

_____

_____

_____

_____

_____

_____

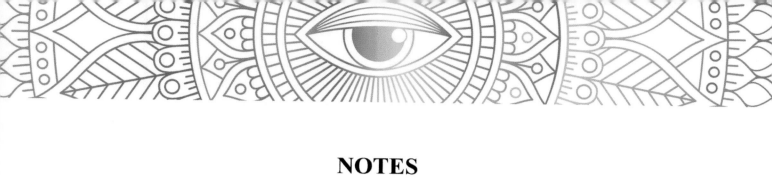

NOTES

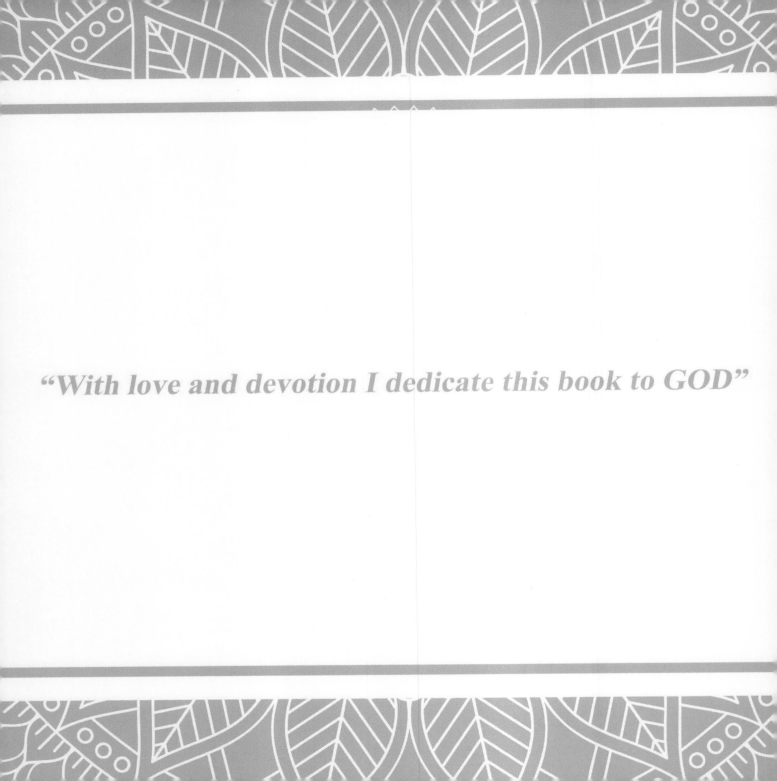

"With love and devotion I dedicate this book to GOD"

12/2/

Printed in Great
Britain
by Amazon